The case for FAITH

FOR KIDS

P9-DTC-558

To Abigail Joy Morrow.
A gift of God's grace.
—LS

Other books in the Lee Strobel series for kids

The Case For Christ For Kids
The Case For A Creator For Kids
Off My Case For Kids

The Case for FAITH

FOR KIDS

Lee Strobel

with ROB SUGGS

zonderkidz

WILLOW
Willow Creek Resources

ZONDERVAN.COM/
AUTHORTRACKER

The children's group of Zondervan

www.zonderkidz.com

The Case for Faith for Kids
Copyright © 2006 by Lee Strobel
Illustrations copyright © 2006 by The Zondervan Corporation

Requests for information should be addressed to:
Grand Rapids, Michigan 49530

Library of Congress Cataloging-in-Publication Data

Strobel, Lee, 1952-
   The case for faith for kids / by Lee Strobel with Rob Suggs.
      p. cm.
   ISBN-13: 978-0-310-71146-9 (softcover)
   ISBN-10: 0-310-71146-0 (softcover)
1. Apologetics--Juvenile literature. I. Suggs, Rob. II. Title.
BT1103.S77 2006
239--dc22
                                                            2005034022

All Scripture quotations, unless otherwise noted, are taken from the Holy Bible: New International Reader's Version®. NIrV®. Copyright © 1995, 1996, 1998 by International Bible Society. Used by permission of Zondervan. All rights reserved.

Scripture quotations marked NIV are from the Holy Bible, New International Version®. NIV®. Copyright © 1973, 1978, 1984 by International Bible Society. Used by permission of Zondervan. All rights reserved.

Holy Bible, New Living Translation. Scripture quotations marked (NLT) are taken from the Holy Bible, New Living Translation, copyright © 1996. Used by permission of Tyndale House Publishers, Inc., Wheaton, IL 60189 USA. All rights reserved.

Scripture quotations marked NCV are taken from the New Century Version. Copyright © 1987, 1988, 1991 by Word Publishing, a division of Thomas Nelson, Inc. Used by permission. All rights reserved.

All rights reserved. No part of this publication may be reproduced, stored in a retrieval system, or transmitted in any form or by any means — electronic, mechanical, photocopy, recording, or any other — except for brief quotations in printed reviews, without the prior permission of the publisher.

Editor: Kristen Tuinstra
Cover Design: Sarah Jongsma and Holli Leegwater
Interior Art Direction: Sarah Jongsma and Kristen Tuinstra
Interior design: Sarah Jongsma
Composition: Ruth Bandstra
Illustrations: Dan Brawner
Photography: Synergy Photographic

Printed in the United States of America

06 07 08 09 10 • 12 11 10 9 8 7 6 5 4

TABLE of CONTENTS

INTRODUCTION:

Any Questions?   6

CHAPTER 1:

Why Would a Good God Allow Bad Things?   16

CHAPTER 2:

Does Science Mean Miracles Can't Happen?   32

CHAPTER 3:

How Do You Make Sense of Jesus?   40

CHAPTER 4:

Can Other Religions Get You into Heaven?   52

CHAPTER 5:

Can You Have Doubts and Still Be a Christian?   64

EPILOGUE:

The Beginning: Where to Next?   76

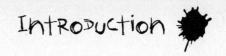

Any Questions?

Hey, do you like questions?

Questions are cool. They come in several flavors. Of course, there are the boring questions:

> Who was the thirteenth president of the United States?
>
> What is the state bird of Montana?

> Then there are those corny questions called riddles:
>
> Why did the chicken cross the playground?
>
> Answer: To get to the other *slide*.

There are also the head-scratching, noggin-tickling questions:

Why do people drive on a parkway but park on a driveway?

Why does "after dark" occur after light?

Why are whales still chubby after all that swimming?

Why don't sheep shrink in the rain?

Why do cameras have round lenses but take square pictures?

Why does night fall but day break?

Why is one of the hottest dishes called "chili"?

Why are many people afraid of heights, but no one is afraid of widths?

Those questions probably have answers, but who cares? They're more interesting the way they are, don't you think?

Then there are questions that *do* have answers. For example, do you ever stand on the beach and wonder how the moon way up *there* causes all those waves way down *here*? Or how long it would take to travel to another galaxy?

You could get those answers without much problem. That's why there's science. The kind of science called *physics* would tell you about the moon and tides. *Astronomy* would tell you about how long to plan for an intergalactic vacation.

Big-league questions

Then there are those questions that everyone wonders about at some time or another:

How did this world get here?

Is there a God?

Which religion is true?

In case you're interested, a book called *The Case for a Creator* worked on the God question. Another one called *The Case for Christ* covered questions about Jesus, such as: Was he really the Son of God? Could he really have risen from the dead?

This book is filled with big-league questions about believing in God and following Christ. Even a lot of Christians wonder about these noggin-nibblers:

If God is good, why does he let bad things happen in the world?

Do miracles happen or does science prove they are impossible?

Is Jesus the only way to get into heaven? What about other religions?

If I have questions or doubts, does that mean I'm not a Christian?

> Herbivorous: an animal that only eats plants. They're vegetarians—no burgers for them!

Why ask in the first place?

Those are some brain-drainers, and that's a ... well, a no-brainer. People ask these questions all the time, and why shouldn't they? The answers are very important. It's only natural that folks would wonder.

One more question: Should people who already believe in God ask for answers? If they wonder, for instance, whether God is really fair, does that mean they don't trust God enough? Should they just ignore the tough stuff and go on believing in God?

No, because questions are too pesky to let us do that. They have a way of hanging around like stray cats in your neighborhood. If you pay even a little bit of attention to a stray, he'll keep showing up at your door. If you pay a little attention to an important question, it'll keep showing up in your mind.

Here's an example. *Don't think of a green-striped hippo.* Go ahead—try not to think of a massive, blubbery, herbivorous, four-toed aquatic artiodactyl mammal with lime green racing stripes. Here is some blank space for you to spend *not thinking* about that.

See? Before, it was easy not to think of one. But once you read those words, *green-striped hippo*, there you go. The more you try not to think of one, the more he makes himself at home inside your brain.

> Artiodactyl: hoofed mammals with an even number of toes. Animals like cows, deer, sheep, camels, goats, and hippopotamuses. (Even green-striped hippos!)

So whether you believe in God or not, it's a pretty good idea to give these questions some thought. Look at it this way: people have worked on these riddles for thousands of years, and they haven't proved yet that God isn't alive. So what do you have to lose?

Not your faith. It's like a muscle that just becomes stronger the more you put it to work. Proverbs 18:17 says, "The first one to tell his case seems right. Then someone else comes forward and questions him." That's just a fancy way of saying it's important to carefully ask the right questions to get the right clues—don't be too quick to jump to conclusions. Then you can make up your mind what the truth is.

Ask. Search. Knock.

Jesus said this: "Ask, and it will be given to you. Search, and you will find. Knock, and the door will be opened to you. Everyone who asks will receive. He who searches will find. The door will be opened to the one who knocks" (Matthew 7:7–8).

Ask, search, and knock. Why?

Imagine trying to find an old friend who moved away from the neighborhood. How would you go about it? First, you would *ask*. "Anybody know where my friend's new house is?" Maybe someone at school would say, "I heard that kid lives over near the park now."

What would you do next? You would *search*. Maybe you'd get on your bike and ride to the park to look for your friend. Finally, what would you do when you found the right house? You would *knock*. Then you could see your friend face-to-face.

1. Ask
2. Search
3. Knock

That's why you ask questions about God. It's a way of finding him for yourself. Asking leads you to search for him more actively, and searching for him makes it possible to meet him.

Remember, even though it's important to ask questions about God to find him, he is always searching for you.

In this verse, God's talking: "When you look for me with all your heart, you will find me" (Jeremiah 29:13). That means to seek with your best effort.

That sounds like a good idea. It's time to really go after these questions. If you ask and think and search for the answers with all your heart, maybe you'll finally discover that every answer leads to God himself. Because, as Saint Augustine said, "all truth is God's truth."

Enough chit-chat. Time to get this show on the road. Tighten your thinking cap, march boldly to the next page, and prepare yourself to do some thinking and maybe even have some fun doing it. You're going to tackle five big-time questions, one by one. That's the plan.

Any questions?

CASE NOTES

{
_____

_____

_____

_____

_____

_____

_____

_____

_____

_____

_____

_____

_____

_____

_____

_____

_____
}

chapter 1

Why Would a Good God Allow Bad Things?

Early on August 29, 2005, Hurricane Katrina hit the Gulf Coast of the United States.

People in the city of New Orleans, Louisiana, were on alert. At first, it seemed as if the winds had done little damage. But the next morning, the storm walls called levees burst. Seawater, swirling wildly from the storm, quickly washed across the city. Hundreds of thousands of people lost their homes and had to flee the city. But some could not leave, because they were sick, handicapped, elderly, or didn't have transportation.

Many people died from the tragic flooding. Survivors flocked to the Louisiana Superdome, the enclosed stadium that had been built for games and fun. It soon became a crowded place of pain and panic. No one had enough water or food. There were no working bathrooms. Families were separated in the confusion.

Then came more tragedy along America's Gulf Coast, this time caused not by wind or water but by people. Criminals showed up on the flooded streets, breaking into buildings and stealing all they could carry. There were violent attacks, some against soldiers and rescuers who came to help. People fought viciously for seats on the buses in order to escape a city of terror that had once been home, a vacation destination, and a place of good food and parties.

There were also heroes who helped others in need of food and shelter. Did you know military troops and volunteers from all over the country traveled down to the Gulf to help clean up the city, hand out food and water, and do lots of other things? The helpers spent many sleepless nights and went without a lot to help in any way they could.

Have you heard about a disaster like Katrina, the tsunami of 2004, or perhaps some fire or accident in your town? Did you see pictures on television? How did you feel when you saw the pictures or heard the stories? Why?

People all over the world began to ask questions. How could *nature* be so cruel? How could *people* behave with even more cruelty at the very worst time?

And where was God when he was needed most? Wasn't he watching out for the world? Couldn't he have stopped the storm? Couldn't he have protected innocent victims from flooding and criminals?

An ancient question

Ever since the earth has had people living on it, these great questions have been asked: Where is God when bad things happen? Why won't he protect people from disaster? Why doesn't he punish the bad people? Deep thinkers call these questions the problem of evil.

They wonder why there is evil at all if the world is guarded by a God who cares about you.

If there is a good God, why do bad things happen?

That last question really takes some tough thinking. A Greek philosopher named Epicurus asked it more than two thousand years ago. It seemed to him that if God and evil are both in the world, then God should use his powers to eliminate it. If he doesn't, the philosopher asked, why doesn't he? Does he lack the desire or does he lack the strength?

That's a tough one! Christians believe God is as good as it is possible to be, *and* as strong as it is possible to be. But if Epicurus were here, he would reply, "Then why does he let bad things happen in the world?"

Problem of evil: questions people ask when bad things happen. The questions are about why God didn't save or help people when they were in trouble.

How would you answer his question? This one's harder than math!
For now, just try to understand
what Epicurus (and many other
people throughout the ages) asked.
As you continue your journey
throughout this book, you'll learn
the best answers for these questions. Fair enough?

Q4U:

When you think of God, do you think more of power
or love? Why?

God and cheaters

You don't need a hurricane to make this question important. Imagine you're sitting in your desk
at school when you see Cheater Chad, that kid over
in the second row sneaking his test answers from a
tiny piece of paper in his watchband. Cheating really

bugs you. On top of that, Chad has all the latest video games, and his parents give him everything he wants.

Then you think of Janet, who sits in the back row. A hard worker, she's nice to everyone. But she comes from a poor family; she owns just two sets of school clothes. Yet Janet is such a nice girl.

After awhile, you begin to wonder why life works out like that. Sometimes the least deserving kids have the best setup. Again, what about God? If he has the power, why doesn't he give Janet the break she deserves—and maybe even teach Cheater Chad a lesson?

A man named Jeremiah asked God about this deal. "But now I would like to speak with you about whether you are being fair. Why are sinful people successful? Why do those who can't be trusted have an easy life?" (Jeremiah 12:1).

Q4U:

What kinds of "unfair" things have you noticed at school or in the neighborhood? Why do you think some people do wrong things but don't get caught?

Ask the expert

Peter Kreeft is a smart man—he teaches philosophy at Boston College. He has done a lot of reading and a lot of thinking about the problem of evil. Imagine you're a reporter trying to stump him with some tough questions.

You: *Peter! What's up? Why would God create evil in the first place?*

PK: *The "first place"? You mean the world, the universe, or …*

You: *Don't dodge the question!*

PK: *Well, my answer would be that God didn't create evil.*

You: *Okay, then who did?*

PK: *We did. By that I mean that God made people. And when he did, he gave them the ability to make decisions in life. That's called "free choice."*

You: *But what about evil?*

PK: *Evil is what happens when people use their free choice in the wrong way. People can choose to love, but they often choose to hurt each other instead. That's what evil is: the decision to do the wrong thing. God doesn't make that decision—we do.*

You: *You're not getting off that easy. Why didn't God make us unable to hate or to hurt?*

PK: *Do you play with dolls?*

You: *Hey! I'm asking the questions here. Besides, it's none of your ...*

PK: *Let's say you have a doll with a little button that makes the doll say, "I love you." Over and over. Is that a great toy or what?*

You: *No way! It's boring!*

PK: *Exactly. If God had made us with no choice, we would be like plastic dolls that couldn't do anything but say, "I love you," over and over. That's not really love because we'd be forced to say it. But we have no buttons. We choose to obey God or not. When we decide to please him because we want to, not because we have to—well, that means something. God doesn't care about dolls, but about real people who make real choices.*

You: *Sort of like when I clean up my room without being asked?*

PK: *Good point. I hear it's really messy today, by the way. Smelly gym socks don't belong on the floor.*

The choice is yours

Professor Kreeft is saying that if you could *only* do good stuff, you would be like a robot—just a lifeless toy that God was playing with.

Think of it another way. Why play soccer? If you play actual games, you could lose! But you do it because the fun makes it worth it, right? If you knew for sure that you would win *every* single game, would winning mean as much or feel as good? Of course not.

People can hurt God's feelings, Professor K says. God made people that way because he wanted real, thinking friends instead of boring dolls or robots. Friendship is worth the risk of disappointment just as soccer is worth the risk of losing. So according to Professor K, God created *choice*. People came up with the evil part.

Okay. Evil is something people do. But wait just a minute! What about the *other* kind of evil? Some evil is not personal, but *natural*—that is, brought about by nature. There are hurricanes, earthquakes, famines, and diseases that make innocent people suffer. Nobody chooses a disaster. So what's up with that?

Diseases and disasters

Some of those deep thinkers feel that natural disasters such as Hurricane Katrina raise much tougher questions about God because people seem to suffer for no good reason. You can't just blame people.

Christians find a consistent answer to this question in the Bible. God's children were actually perfect in every way before they chose to disobey him. Disobeying is called "sin." Sinning caused humans to be imperfect, and thus also caused the earth to be imperfect. God said, "I am putting a curse on the ground because of what you did" (Genesis 3:17). Through poor choices, people and the world were damaged. Therefore, there are diseases and disasters.

One Christian thinker, Cliffe Knechtle, put it this way: "When we humans told God to shove off, he partially honored our request. Nature began to revolt. The earth was cursed. Genetic breakdown and disease began. Pain and death became part of the human experience."

All of God's creation, therefore, is hurting. It is "groaning," according to Romans 8:22. That's the bad news. The good news is, things are going to get better! "All creation anticipates the day when it will join God's children in glorious freedom from death and decay" (Romans 8:21 NLT). What does that mean? God has a plan to restore perfection to both the people and the planet.

Payback or proving ground?

One day Jesus and his friends met a man who had been blind since birth. They began to discuss whether his blindness was God's punishment for the man's wrong behavior, or whether it was payback for something his parents had done. (In those days, many people believed that disabilities were punishment for wrongdoing.)

Jesus said both views were wrong. It was actually "so that God's work could be shown" (John 9:3). Now there's an idea! No one likes problems, but you can look at them as a chance to show the difference God can make in your problems.

You might want to read about Helen Keller, who showed just how many wonderful things one blind and deaf person can do in serving God.

Evil, then, is not just a problem—it's an opportunity to make something good out of the situation.

So why doesn't God do something now?

There is at least one good reason God doesn't snap a heavenly finger and make all the bad things go away. It's easier to understand when you think about how parents raise their children.

Mom watches Timmy every moment when Timmy is a baby. But as Timmy gets a little older, she allows him to play outside— even out of her sight when he reaches a certain age. What if he falls down and skins a knee? He just might, but Mom knows that Timmy eventually must learn how to care for himself, and she will hear him if he calls for her. Besides, what would Timmy's life be like if his mother followed him every-where, protecting him even when he became a teen-ager? Timmy wouldn't like it!

What if your parents never let you ride a bicycle because they knew that you would take a few tumbles while learning? If they want you to have all the fun of bike-riding, they have to let you experience a few bumps and bruises.

God allows people to suffer sometimes because there is a lesson to learn—and because of one other cool idea found in the Bible, in Romans chapter 8. Wait'll you see this one!

All for the best

Here's one amazing verse. It says that no matter what happens, God is going to bring something good out of it for his followers! *Can he do that?* Well, after all, he is God.

> *We know that in all things God works for the good of those who love him.*
>
> —*Romans 8:28*

As amazing as it seems, this happens so often in life. The Gulf Coast hurricane is one example. Within a few days of the tragedy, people all over the United States were offering to help. Some of them opened their homes for victims of the disaster to come stay with them. People gave food, clothing, money, and new houses. Some kids gave up all their birthday presents to let the money be used for helping those in need.

Whenever bad things happen, good people seem to come from every direction, ready to help. Maybe God sends them. Maybe he's not ignoring people's problems after all.

Have you ever helped people in need? Have you heard stories of people who helped after a disaster? How did that make you feel?

Yeah, but evil is *still* unfair!

Still worried about tragedies and innocent children who die of starvation? You should be! There is no simple answer for the question of why innocent people suffer sometimes. The ideas in this chapter help, but that doesn't make evil any less evil. Just because you might see how God works does *not* mean that disasters and diseases are good in any way.

It *does* mean that no matter how dark the world may become, God's light is brighter still. The Bible also says there will be a time when there will be no more darkness or evil at all—in human nature or the world of nature.

"We are looking forward to a new heaven and a new earth. Godliness will make its home there. All of this is in keeping with God's promise" (2 Peter 3:13).

CHAPTER 2

DOES SCIENCE MEAN MIRACLES CAN'T HAPPEN?

"Hi there, Levi. How was your day? Eat all your lunch?"

"Nope, Mom. Shared it with a few friends."

"Well, that was nice. Which friends would they be?"

"Don't know all their names."

"*All* their names? You had one fish sandwich. How many friends did you share it with?"

"Five thousand."

Silence.

"Levi, what have we told you about telling fibs?"

"I'm not fibbing! Folks were hungry. Teacher said to share. I shared."

"Levi, that comes out to —um, five thousand eaters, half a crumb per person. No way."

"Way. Actually, everyone chowed down until they were stuffed."

"Leeeeeeeeviii …"

"Um … Mom?"

"What now?"

"Where should I put this basket of leftovers?"

There wasn't much science back in the day (this made-up story was based on a true one about Jesus that you can read in Matthew 14). Even so, Levi's mom understood that sandwiches answer to certain physical laws, and sandwiches are pretty law-abiding in that regard. Meaning, you could split a fish sandwich only so many ways.

These days, people take science for granted. You can watch something on your television set as it is happening on the other side of the world. You can fly through the sky in an airplane. A century or two ago, such things would have seemed greater miracles than five thousand dudes sharing a trout-burger. But you know that television and air flight are just matters of science.

But that raises another big-league question. If science can explain so many things, doesn't that mean there are no real miracles?

The reason that's such a big question is if there is only science (natural) and nothing miraculous (supernatural), then where does that leave God? You can't see him through a microscope or a telescope, after all. In the Bible, he used miracles to show he was real. So what's the deal? Can miracles happen? And if not, does that mean there is no God?

Or is there some way both science and miracles can be true?

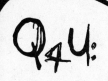

Do you think miracles happen today? If you could ask God to perform one miracle, what would it be? Why?

Ask the philosopher

Put your reporter hat on again. Time to take a little trip.

You're climbing a mountain in the mysterious Himalayas. Snow whips around your body as you try to make your way to the top. The wind howls as you reach the crest, where a philosopher sits—a wise guru, thinking deep thoughts about the meaning of life. His lengthy beard spills around his bare feet, and a hood covers his eyes. His name is Bill Craig.

(Okay. So the mountain stuff and how the guy looks are made up. Bill Craig is a real guy, but he sits in an office studying all day. This book needed a little more mystery and adventure, okay?)

You: Dude. You're a deep guy. A thinking guy. A science guy.

BC: Well, I like to think so.

You: But you're a faith guy too?

BC: Definitely. I believe in Jesus with all my heart.

You: So how did that happen? Jesus is all about miracles and the supernatural, right?

BC: I became a Christian because I cared about Jesus. I have experienced him, just like I would "experience" something in science or regular life. You don't have to have all your questions answered to come to faith. You just have to say, "The weight of the evidence seems to show this is true, so even though I don't have answers to all my questions, I'm going to believe and hope for answers in the long run." That's what happened with me. And the more I've seen the evidence of science and history, the more it has strengthened my faith.

You: Well, if you believe in science, what do you do when the Bible tells you that Jesus fed five thousand people with a little bread and fish?

BC: What I do is figure that if Jesus is God, as he says he is, he can do what he wants. He made the universe, so what's the big deal about feeding a few extra people? Or walking on water? Or rising from the dead, for that matter? God made science, not the other way around.

You: Still, doesn't he have to break the laws of science — mess up his own system — to perform a miracle?

BC: *Not the way I look at it. Let's say an apple is about to fall from the tree. The laws of science (gravity, actually) say it will hit the ground. But I step up and catch the apple. Have I broken the laws of science?*

You: *If so, I won't tattle on you. (You're so funny!)*

BC: *The answer is no, I haven't. I have stepped in and intervened. A miracle is when God steps in and does something in the world. It's supernatural—that means it's not against nature but higher than nature.*

Even though miracles might seem supernatural to us, they aren't to God. They're just part of God's ability to reach out to us.

CASE NOTES

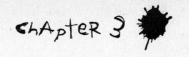

ChApteR 3

How Do You Make
Sense of Jesus?

As you nervously climb back down the mountain, searching for a foothold as the wind rages (just play along, you're on a roll), you carry a piece of paper. That Bill Craig guy handed it to you. You had said, "Okay, Mr. Philosopher, if you're so smart, give me five good reasons to believe in God when science explains so much."

He said, "No problem," and pulled out this handy slip of paper with five points on it. You decided to read it when you got to the bottom of the page—um, the mountain.

Five reasons God makes sense even with science

1. God makes sense of creation.

Many scientists today believe that the universe began with a "big bang." All matter—every particle that existed—was together before exploding outward. The explosion, still in progress, created every star, every planet, and everything else in space.

But what made the bang?

No matter how much scientists discover about that first explosion that brought the universe into being, we must agree that something had to make it happen. It couldn't just come from nothing. After all, whatever begins to exist has a cause. If the universe began to exist at some point in the past, then it must have had a cause. What could that cause have been? God makes the most sense.

(And what caused God to exist? Well, unlike the universe, he never had a beginning, so he doesn't need a cause!)

God has always existed. He never had a beginning, so he doesn't need a cause to exist.

2. God makes sense of the fine details of life.

Scientists are learning a lot about how stuff works in the universe. They're discovering more about how gravity pulls things to earth, what it takes to be able to live and breathe on a planet like ours—things like that.

These same scientists have been amazed at what they have found. For example, a famous scientist named Stephen Hawking figured out that the big bang happened in *exactly, absolutely, precisely* the right way for there to even *be* a universe. If the speed of the bang had been different by one part in a hundred thousand *million million*, the whole thing would have collapsed into a fireball! Who could have fine-tuned the whole thing to make sure that didn't happen?

Or think about this one, worked out by a scientist named P. C. W. Davies. If the force of gravity were weaker *or* stronger by one part in a number we don't have room to write here (10 with one hundred zeros after it!), then there never could have been life on this earth. Imagine someone sprinkling enough salt to cover the entire surface of a football field. There is one specific grain of salt that is the "special" one (though it looks like every other grain of salt). How likely would it be that you could walk out there and select *that very grain* without help? Not much chance, right?

The force of gravity is set at one specific measurement that is even more precise than that. It could have been any other measurement, just like any of those other grains of salt. Could it have just worked out exactly right without someone "helping" to select the right measurement? In other words, who could have fine-tuned the force of gravity? Think about it the next time you drop your ice-cream cone. Who sits at the controls and sets all the dials? God makes sense when you look at the details of life.

Try it yourself!

Got a deck of cards? Build a house with them. Prop up four cards for your walls, then put on a ceiling.

Now that you've mastered a simple shack, try a mansion. Add several more packs of cards. Build some large rooms and make your home seven or eight stories high. Can you do it? How about a skyscraper?

As you can see, you have to be able to balance every single card perfectly in relation to every single other card. Because just when you get everything to barely balance, adding another card throws everything off and makes the whole house fall down—unless you have superhuman balancing skills.

Scientists say the universe is like an almost infinitely high skyscraper of cards, each card (or physical condition) arranged so delicately in relation to every other one that if you pulled out one card, the house would collapse.

The Bible says that Jesus "created everything in heaven and on earth. He created everything that can be seen and everything that can't be seen ... He holds everything together" (Colossians 1:16–17).

3. God makes sense of right and wrong.

Have you ever thought about where "right" and "wrong" come from? Some ideas are opinions, such as whether red is a better color than blue. Everyone knows there are no right or wrong answers for color preference; it just depends on who is being asked. But when it comes to stealing and child abuse, most people all over the world agree that these things are really wrong. Why? Who decides certain things are right or wrong, period?

If you think about it, if there were no God, every idea would just be an opinion. You couldn't say that child abuse or stealing were "just wrong, period." It would be like red or blue, chocolate or vanilla—one answer would be as good as the other.

Once you decide that certain things are always right or always wrong, then what you are saying is that there is something like an "honor code" for the whole world—even for the universe. Does your school have an honor code, telling students how they must behave? Someone had to write it—maybe the principal, the teachers, or a group of parents. Rules don't write themselves. But if the universe has its own "honor code"—that is, its own set of rules saying what is right and what is wrong—then those can't have written themselves, either. Could God be the one who made the rules?

If you were the king of the world, what rules for right and wrong would you set? Make a list, and think about why each rule would be on your list. If God were making the rules for us, which would be most important to him? Why?

4. God makes sense of Jesus.

Remember, the subject for this chapter is miracles. If there is a God, then you have to admit that miracles are really no big deal! After all, someone who made the universe can do anything else he wants.

The claim that Jesus rose from the dead is a good example. That would definitely qualify as a miracle, right? But how do you know it happened? Some people insist that the story of Jesus coming back from the dead is a fairy tale, like the story of the Three Bears or Cinderella.

Here are some facts to consider about the death and resurrection of Jesus:

- Everyone knew where he was buried, and the grave was guarded by Roman soldiers.
- Jesus' friends *and* enemies agreed that the body disappeared in only three days.
- Many people saw and talked with Jesus alive after his death.

- The disciples were certain he had risen from
  the dead—so certain they were willing to give
  their lives for telling others about it.

All of these points were known just a relatively
short time after the events. Anyone who knew these
to be lies could have said so. But instead, thousands of
people began coming forward to become Christians.
Something remarkable surely happened.

If Jesus rose from the dead, then the work of God is
the best explanation.

5. God makes sense of our personal experiences.

What if your friend told you that the president of
the United States was in the next room? It might be
pretty hard to believe, but you could check it out.
You could listen at the door—could you recognize
his voice? You could ask others in the room if they
knew anything about the president visiting your
home. But what would be the smartest way to find
out? Go and see!

When it comes to the question of God, many people
have gone and seen. They have sought God and, they
claim, became his friend. This includes many scientists. When you know someone as a friend, you have
no more questions about whether they are real. This is
still the most convincing point of all.

Who is at the door?

As you've seen, scientists and other people have gone looking for God. But the good news is that he comes looking for people first. He is looking for you too. How can you know him?

Jesus said, "Here I am! I stand at the door and knock. If any of you hears my voice and opens the door, I will come in and eat with you. And you will eat with me" (Revelation 3:20). That means he expects you to listen for his knock in everyday life. Letting him in means accepting his friendship.

That's when the really cool miracles begin!

Q4U:

Do you have a friendship with God? How is it like other friendships? How is it different? What are some ways that you can make your relationship with God into an even deeper and closer friendship?

CASE NOTES

{
_____

_____

_____

_____

_____

_____

_____

_____

_____

_____

_____

_____

_____

_____

_____

_____

_____
}

CAn OtheR ReLiGions Get You into HeAven?

Imagine a giant pyramid, a little like the Great Pyramid of Egypt. But this one has more than four sides. And each side has steps leading upward to its peak, where all the lines come together. One side is marked "Christianity" at the bottom. Many people are eagerly climbing those steps. The next side is marked "Hinduism." It too claims a huge number of devoted climbers. After that comes the side marked "Buddhism," then one marked "Islam." There are many other sides too, though they are smaller and have fewer people climbing their steps.

At the top of the pyramid, God waits with a big smile. He shakes each person's hand as they reach the top, and he gives that person a ticket to heaven.

But a Buddhist says, "Wait a minute! I did a lot of thinking and reading before choosing my side of the pyramid. I gotta know—was Buddhism the best way or not?"

God shrugs and says, "Oh, six of one, half a dozen of the other, ya know? All these religions are about the same."

A Christian joins the conversation. "The same? How can that be? I made a comparison, and there were *big* differences."

God says, "Hey, I don't sweat the small stuff. I figure, whatever beliefs work for you are cool with me."

A Muslim says, "But on some of the sides, people were taught that it was right to *kill* for their gods. And some said there's *one* of you, while others said there are a *bunch* of gods. Some said there's one life-time for people on earth, while others said we get a bunch of chances. Are you going to announce the right answers?"

God holds up a hand and says, "Hey, I don't make the rules ... Tickets! Tickets for all!"

> Even though not everyone is a Christian, it's important to show kindness to people of all faiths. In fact, the Bible tells Christians: "Always be prepared to give an answer to everyone who asks you to give a reason for the hope that you have. But do this with gentleness and respect" (1 Peter 3:15 NIV).

Does this seem like a strange picture of God? Sure, it's a little goofy, but many people today hold to some-thing like that view. They think the world's religions are basically equal. They think the differing views of God, the world, and proper behavior aren't worth wor-rying about. They believe that truth is whatever any-one decides it is, like chocolate versus vanilla—and that anyone who claims to have the *right* answer is stuck-up.

So what should you do with the words of Jesus? He is on the record as saying, "I am the way ... No one comes to the Father except through me" (John 14:6). He claims to hold the exclusive ticket to heaven, and he says that everyone must walk on *his* side of the pyramid.

Is that fair? It's a tough question, isn't it? Is there only one way to heaven? Many ways? No way? Is the answer important?

That's the ticket!

Imagine you want to go to that big, new theme park, the one with the wild roller coaster called the Nauseator. Since it's Saturday, tickets are sold out, but there are various people walking around outside the gates selling pre-bought tickets. You and your friends are bargaining with some of them, trying to get the best price on tickets.

As you read the pyramid story, what do you think about its view of God and religion? What seems right or wrong about it to you?

But you've heard that some of the tickets are fakes! They look real, but they are clever copies of the real thing. At the park gate, the ticket-takers will point special scanners at the tickets and reveal them to be worthless—and some kids will go home disappointed and missing a bunch of dollars.

You'd have to agree that with amusement park tickets, it's important to know the real ones from the fakes. The same can be applied to religion. Isn't it an even bigger deal with religions other than Christianity? Is it a good idea to simply assume that all the "tickets" to heaven are authentic? And if so, how can you tell which one will get you in the front gate?

All created equal?

Some people say that all religions are about the same, but that's actually not true. Ready to play the reporter again? Time to talk to an expert on world religions and find out why. His name is Ravi Zacharias, and he grew up in India with friends who were Hindu and Buddhist.

RZ: *Don't forget Sikh.*

You: *Sorry to hear that. I hope you'll be feeling better soon.*

RZ: *No, Sikh. It sounds like seek, and it's a religion related to Hinduism.*

You: *I knew that. Dr. Z, what's really different about some of these faith "labels"? Isn't it like buying the same kind of medicine under different brand names at the drugstore? Like six different brands of aspirin?*

RZ: *Not at all. With medicine, you can look on the side and see what's contained in every pill or dose. If you "check the contents" of religions, you find they are entirely different inside. When I'm sick, I want exactly the right medicine, not just whatever happens to be on the shelf.*

You: *Sorry to hear that. I hope you feel better soon.*

RZ: *For the last time, I'm not Sikh—um, sick. Now you've got me doing it! Listen, Christians, Jews, and Muslims claim that there is one God. Hindus say there are many.*

*Buddhists and atheists say there is none. Christians say
Jesus is the Son of God, but Muslims say God has no
son. They can't all be right, can they? When people give
conflicting answers to the same question, someone must
be wrong while someone else may be right. But it would
be irrational to say that all the answers were right. How
many fingers are on my hand?*

You: *Let me see, one, two … six. No, five.*

RZ: *Is this a matter of opinion?*

You: *No. Five fingers.*

RZ: *Why should the number of gods be a matter of
opinion?*

You: *What about that story of the blind men and the elephant? One sat in front, felt the trunk, and said, "An
elephant is like a snake." Another sat by the side, felt a
leg, and said, "An elephant is like a thick tree." A third
felt the ears and said, "You're both wrong. An elephant
is like a fan." Aren't the religions sort of like different
sides of an elephant?*

RZ: *In a way. But the blind men are all wrong. Someone
with sight can see what the elephant is. He knows
the truth. And Jesus Christ has made it clear that the
eternal truths of God may be known. Jesus Christ is
the centerpiece. In him, all of truth came together. So
while there may be aspects of truth elsewhere, the sum
total of truth is in Christ. So should we go around cor-
recting all the people who disagree with us? We must*

*always be very careful! When speaking of matters
that are important to people, such as belief in God, we
need to be gentle and understanding. Some people like
Christ, but they don't like Christians very much. Our
failure to be gentle may be why.*

You: *So we should pretty much mind our own business?*

RZ: *I didn't say that. It's important to tell the truth—we
just should do it gently. We need to show people we
really do care about them. We need to build strong
friendships so that we'll have the chance to sit down
and talk over these life-changing ideas with them.*

You: *Sounds good. Anything else people should do?*

RZ: *Yes! Live out what you believe. Show people through
your life that Jesus is not just an idea, but he's real
and we can know him personally.*

Christians should be humble in talking with others about God. Someone who knows a lot about the Bible, D.T. Niles, said, "We're just one beggar telling another beggar where to find food."

Okay, so why isn't everybody a Christian?

Here's a question to consider: If Christianity is the true religion, why doesn't everybody find that out and switch to Christianity or become a Christian?

Following Jesus means learning to live unselfishly, to pray for enemies, and to avoid striking back at people who hurt us. If a friend told you that for those reasons, Christianity wasn't worth it, what would you tell him or her?

For one thing, of course, many people are born in countries where certain religions have been popular for thousands of years. There are many Buddhists in China and Japan; many Hindus in India and surrounding countries; many Muslims in Middle Eastern countries. In the United States, more than eight out of ten people say they're Christians. So people tend to adopt the religions of their homelands.

Still, in today's world, where there is more travel and more discussion between people from different cultures, people take new forms of faith at times. Missionaries, including Christian ones, are active in spreading their beliefs to other countries.

Some people reject Christianity because it's demanding. Jesus calls people to be unselfish, and to treat others as if they were more important than themselves. Some people don't want to try living that way.

What about people who haven't heard?

One more difficult question. People often ask if it's fair for Christians, and Christians alone, to be allowed into heaven. What if a child is born in a country where few people are Christians? What if she lives her whole life and never hears about Jesus? Would it be fair to exclude her from heaven? One answer might…

RZ: *Excuse me. May I reply? This is a biggie!*

You: *Only if you promise to stop sneaking up on me like that, Dr. Z. Go ahead and do your thing.*

RZ: *Well, first of all, remember that missionaries travel all over the world to be sure that people hear about Jesus. Also, in Romans 1:19 – 20, the Bible tells us that since the beginning of the world, the true God has made himself plain to all people so that they would have a chance to know him. In Acts 17:26 – 27, it says that God carefully placed people where he wanted them to live so that they would seek him. And finally, there is this wonderful verse in Jeremiah 29:13 in which God says, "When you look for me with all your heart, you will find me."*

You: It sounds like God cares very much about every human being.

RZ: There are two or three things we can be very certain about with God. One is that he is fair. Another is that he loves everyone with a love that never lets up. He has placed a special need in the heart of each one of us—the need for him. It's like being thirsty. There is only one thing you can do to get rid of your thirst, and that is to drink. There is only one way to fill our need for God, and that is to find him. And remember: he's not hiding from us! He wants us to know him personally.

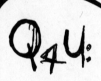

God says that if you seek him with all your heart, you will find him. What are some ways of seeking him? Do you feel a need for God inside you, as described by Dr. Z? Explain or think about your feeling.

CHAPTER 5

CAN YOU HAVE DOUBTS AND STILL BE A CHRISTIAN?

Pretend you have a friend named Jason. You want his opinion about what you have been reading so far in this book. Imagine he's been reading this book too.

You: *What do you think about all this, Jason? Do you have a question?*

J: *Not one question. A lot of them. Or at least ... What I'm trying to say is that I'm still not too sure about all this God stuff. Even after all these ideas and experts and stuff, I don't feel like my faith is very strong.*

> You: *Jason, most people are like you at one time or another.*
> *The truth is that if it were easy to have faith, it wouldn't*
> *be called "faith." It would be called "being sure."*
>
> J: *Okay, so I like to be sure. Is that so wrong? If I'm on a*
> *skateboard, I like to be sure the wheels aren't going to*
> *fly off when I'm cruising at high speed. If I'm going to*
> *make a big deal about God in my life, why shouldn't I*
> *be sure about that too?*
>
> You: *Good point! Think about that one.*

Another word for faith is *trust*. Some things are easy to trust—that the sun will come up tomorrow, or that doing homework will help your grades. Seeing is believing, and you've seen those things happen and built your trust on what you've seen.

> Commitment (kuh-MIT-ment): Another part of trust is *commitment.* This means agreeing to do something in the future, like your homework or reading the Bible.

But when it comes to questions about God, people are asked to be "sure of what we hope for ... being certain of what we do not see" (Hebrews 11:1). That's hard to do, isn't it?

Jesus had a friend named Thomas who was just like Jason. Even after his friends had told him that Jesus had risen from death, he needed to see with his own eyes before he would believe. When Thomas did see Jesus face-to-face, he bowed before him in faith. Jesus said, "You believe because you see me. Those who believe without seeing me will be truly happy" (John 20:29 NCV).

Truly happy. Cool. Jesus seems to be saying that life is good when you can believe without demanding absolute proof. In other words, faith is an awesome gift.

But does that mean believing anything and everything? Of course not. Jesus isn't suggesting that you'll be truly happy if you convince yourself that all your teachers at school are aliens from outer space, or that you can learn to fly by flapping your arms. True faith is about managing to believe what already happens to be true. It's a step taken in the same direction that the evidence points.

You look at your skateboard. Will the wheels come flying off if you trust it at high speeds? It's one thing to just hope so. It's another thing when your older brother, good with fix-it stuff, says, "Hey, I've checked it. The wheel axles are solid!"

That's more than just hope. That's moving ahead based on trusting solid evidence.

So faith is cool. It's based on something *solid*—the evidence you already learned that points to God being real. (Rembember the Big Five points made by Dr. Craig?) But doubt is *not* uncool—it actually makes you work on your faith. Make sense? It's all about learning to live with both. It's time to figure out how to do that.

What faith isn't

Some people believe that if they have faith, they should *feel* something. They think that if God lives inside them, they should feel different—like feeling full after dinner or feeling cold in the winter. They wonder why they don't "feel" their faith more.

But feeling full or cold is a *physical* feeling. Some feelings are emotions, and they can be fussy or not quite right at times! They change like the weather, and sometimes they don't agree with your *deeper* feelings. Imagine

Q4U:

Can you remember when someone fooled you by getting you to believe something that wasn't true? How can you decide whether to believe someone's claim?

having a terrible argument with your sister outdoors. Right at that moment, you feel like you could clobber her! But imagine that ten seconds later, your sister almost steps in front of a speeding car. Your emotions would quickly change to alarm. You would realize that you love your sister, even when you want to clobber her.

Emotions come and go, and they don't always tell the whole story, do they?

Faith is like love—you can have it without feeling it. You can believe in God even when it feels like he is far away. It's even possible to love God when you're angry with him!

Faith and doubt are friends

It's also true that faith and doubt are not natural enemies. Actually, those two get along pretty well together.

One day a man came to Jesus with a son who needed healing. Jesus told the father that everything is possible for someone who believes. The man said, "I do believe! Help me overcome my unbelief!" (Mark 9:24). Now, there's something—a man who says that he believes and he doesn't believe. That's kind of like … well, pretty much everybody. It's not that people have *no* faith. They just want God to help them with those little unfaithful parts inside them.

If you could ask God one question about spiritual things, what question would you ask? If you could name one area where you have some doubts, what would it be?

You will find that there are many people who have been Christians for a lot of years. They continue in their faith, and they continue in their doubts too.

Jason: *Excuse me.*

You: *Oh—Jason! I almost forgot you!*

Jason: *I noticed. I wanted to ask how come those old and wise Christian types still have doubts. Shouldn't they have patched up all the holes in their faith by now?*

You: *That would be like getting so muscular, you didn't need to lift any more weights. You could always be at least a little stronger, right? Same way with believing. Doubt is the "heavy lifting" of faith. That is, faith is a kind of spiritual muscle you have to exercise by stretching it, working on it, and hammering it until it's tough. Doubt does that.*

Jason: *Um, I don't get it.*

You: *Well, let's say you doubt that Jesus rose from the dead. So you go and do a lot of reading about it. If you can disprove it, you'll be the first guy in two thousand years to succeed. If you can't, well, you'll have stronger faith! You've just pumped some spiritual iron.*

Work those muscles!

Okay, so doubt can be like a faith workout. It's kind of heavy and tiring, but it makes you stronger. What are some guidelines for a bout with doubt? Or to put the question another way: Are there more ways you can get stronger in your faith?

Glad you asked that question!

1. Take one giant step.

Sometimes people believe something mostly because they *want* to—or they disbelieve it for the same reason. If someone tells you that your best friend said something bad about you, you don't want to believe it. You might choose then and there to disbelieve. Of course, you'll want to discover the truth by asking some questions.

But you see the point: the desire to believe something has an influence over what people end up believing and doing. You can begin in your faith by making a decision to believe. Does that mean a blind, unthinking decision? Should you put the names of the world's religions in a hat, pick one out at random, and make a decision to follow it?

No way! Faith is never blind. Someone once defined faith in this way: "Faith is walking to the edge of all the light that you have and taking one more step." That step comes when you make a conscious decision to go forward. If the step you're taking is in the same direction that the evidence is pointing—as with Christianity— then that's a logical and rational direction to go.

2. Follow the faithful.

You: *Yo, Jason.*
Jason: *Reporting for duty.*

You: *What do you think about taking that giant step?*

Jason: *Um ... Sorry, I missed that one. I was off lifting weights. Thanks for reminding me, dude! I about cramped my left triceps big-time. Feel this knot ...*

You: *Later, okay? Question: If you want to build your faith, where should you go, other than to the fitness center?*

Jason: *Um, I'd say ... off to some place in the wilderness, like, to meditate? Maybe in a cave?*

You: *Well, no, actually. If you wanted to learn to surf, wouldn't you go to the ocean? If you wanted to learn mountain-climbing, wouldn't you go to the mountains? If you want to learn more about faith, you should go where the faithful people are.*

Jason: *Man, I blew that one.*

You: *Forget it. Consider it a faith cramp. The point is, it makes sense to hang out with some cool Christian believers if you want to learn more about being a Christian. Find a church you really like, one with a good youth program. Also, there are a lot of great books, videos, even websites you can be loading into your mind.*

Remember, just doing those things won't make you strong in your faith—just like being in a garage won't make you a car. But if you have already made a decision to pursue your faith (which really means pursuing God), then these are things you can do to help your faith become a little stronger every day.

The faith workout

Use this handy list to establish the right elements to help you grow in your faith each day. You might want to ask some adults to help you fill out certain sections, like the ones on books and music.

These are some people I respect who can help me grow in my faith:

_____

_____

_____

_____

Books to feed my brain:

_____

_____

_____

Music to feed my ears:

_____

_____

_____

Websites for faith-types:

_____

_____

_____

Other stuff I want to write:

_____

_____

_____

The Beginning:
Where to Next?

Get it?

What's just above—those five words—that's what!
Did you get it?

It says, "The Beginning." Get it? This part of the book
is usually called "The End," but not in this book! Here
it's called "The Beginning." Isn't that a riot?

You don't think so?

Okay, well, maybe you can make up a better title
for the last chapter. Just cross out our title and write
in your own. Because you know what? That's kind of
what this part of the book is about anyway: cross-
ing out stuff and writing in your own. You're talking
about questions, answers, growth, and *faith*.

In these pages you worked through some of the big questions people have about believing in God. The questions were set up and knocked down. You learned a lot about what experts have studied and learned about faith and God. In every case, these people have built a stronger faith and happier lives.

Now it's time for you to start your own journey. That's why this chapter is called "The Beginning: Where to Next?" Because books run out of pages. Because writers run out of words. Because the time comes when you have to take the ball and run with it.

So, where to now?

Multiple choice

What are your options? Well, there are a bunch. You could join any of the following groups:

Deniers, who reject the whole idea of God.

Delayers, who believe in God, but they never get started on the journey.

Departers, who start the journey but never get too far.

Delighters, who get going and travel with excitement.

You're going to meet a lot of people in your lifetime. A few of them will be Deniers, who chuck the whole idea of God and faith. Deniers say things like, "Why would I need God? I live the way I want," or, "It's all foolish superstition."

There are plenty of Delayers too. When you meet them, they're likely to say something like, "Sure, I suppose there's probably some kind of God out there." But Delayers are in no hurry to set out on the journey to find out for sure. They live very much like the first group, actually.

Departers grab their coats and say, "Sounds great; let's go!" when you invite them on the journey of faith. But they get distracted. They have trouble staying on the path. These are people who believe in God and have a little faith, but they haven't taken it very far.

Finally, there are a few people out there who are Delighters. They are delighted with God. They are

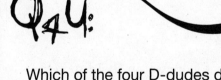

Which of the four D-dudes describes you best? Which category would you like to be a part of? Why?

delighted with their faith. They are delighted when they see new evidence from science and history that makes their faith even stronger. And they delight God too. They believe in the verse that says, "Find your delight in the LORD. Then he will give you everything your heart really wants" (Psalm 37:4). For them, life is a journey of adventure, with something new and exciting every day. Their eyes are set on something in the distance, as if they see a wonderful destination at the end of the road. Listen to what the Bible says about them:

> *What if they had been thinking of the country they had left? Then they could have returned to it. Instead, they longed for a better country. They wanted one in heaven. So God is pleased when they call him their God. In fact, he has prepared a city for them.*
>
> *—Hebrews 11:15–16*

New questions

If you choose to place yourself in that final category—those who travel the journey of faith with delight—you may very well continue to have some questions. But some of the questions will be new ones. You'll have questions such as:

- How can I learn even more about God?
- How can I please him even more?
- How can I invite some of my friends to make the journey with me?

That last question is a good one. Because whenever you discover something really awesome, you are eager to share it with friends. You might even start by sharing this book with a friend. Then you can talk together about some of the ideas in here.

But look! Space is running out. It's time for you to get going. Have a great trip. Enjoy every moment. Bring along your best questions and a good, God-given mind to think them over with. You're going to have a great time, because there's one thing about this trip: It's not just the destination that's fantastic. The journey is wonderful too. It's filled with hope, new friends along the way, and new things to learn all the time. Best of all is realizing that when you get to the end of the trail, all of your questions will be fully answered—by your best friend, God himself.

Check out this excerpt from The Case for a Creator for Kids!

The Case for a CREATOR

FOR KIDS

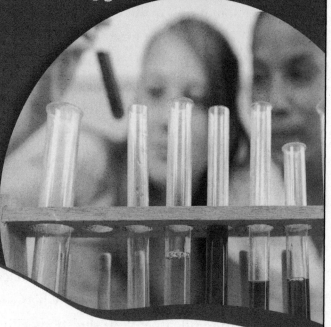

Lee Strobel

with Rob Suggs

zonderkidz

Who Ya Gonna Believe?

There you are sitting in science class at school. You're thinking...

Say, what *are* you thinking? What are your feelings about science in general? Not as cool as a science-fiction movie? More fun than having a cavity drilled? Your true answer is in there somewhere.

Either way, it's science class. And it's an interesting one today, because Mr. Axiom, the science teacher, is starting a new unit on how the world began. You hear something about a Big Bang, and how all the stuff that made up the entire universe was gummed up into one puny little wad before it blew up. And how that stuff is *still* exploding outward, as it has since the beginning.

The story line could use a few aliens and starships, but all in all, it's really pretty cool. The Big Bang doesn't sound too scientific, but again—pretty cool!

Fast-forward a couple of days. Now you're in Sunday school. Mrs. Homily, the teacher, is starting a new unit on the first book of the Bible, called Genesis. She starts with the very first words of Genesis, "In the beginning God created the heavens and the earth."

The kids are kind of nodding along, but you have a big question about all this. Why aren't Mrs. Homily and Mr. Axiom on the same page? They seem to have two completely different stories for the same subject. Mr. Axiom says the universe came from a big explosion; Mrs. Homily claims it came from God. Who's right and who's wrong?

What really bothers you the most is that Mr. Axiom, the science guy, seems to make the best case for his claims. A humongous, long-ago explosion is a pretty wild story, to be honest, but he makes it believable. He gives numbers and details, and tells why the scientists came up with their ideas.

Evidence (EV-eh-dents): proof that something happened.

You've always liked Mrs. Homily. What's weird is that she's only telling you what your parents might have told you all your life: God made everything. You've always liked church and gone along with the program. But you're not a little kid anymore. You're going to be a teenager soon. You're beginning to think things through for yourself. And you're noticing that neither Mrs. Homily nor anyone at church is too concerned about ... well, the *reasons* and the *evidence* for what they're teaching you. Not as much as in science class.

For example, you see a baseball lying in a pile of broken glass next to a window. That's your *evidence* that the baseball broke the window. Better hope that baseball isn't yours!

What do you like or dislike about science? What kinds of science subjects have you enjoyed studying most?

CHAPTER 1

HOW DO YOU FIT THE PIECES TOGETHER?

So you've decided to assemble the whole puzzle for yourself— at least as many pieces as someone your age can handle. Who is right? Science or God? School or church? Both? Neither?

Beginning the search

Get ready to do some detective work. You'll look for clues about how the world got here and whether God had anything to do with it—or whether there is a God in the first place.

But that's not so easy, is it? Since God is supposed to be invisible, and since he would have put this world together a long time ago, how will you get to the truth of the matter?

Well, it's all about detective work. Imagine you're looking for answers about some other question. Pretend there's an elephant on your roof. One day you're leaving for school, and you see the massive fellow sitting there on top of your house. Whoever was in charge of this elephantine act is no longer on the scene. But your mom wants to know how that

elephant got up there. (How to get him down would also be helpful information!) Where would you begin your investigation?

First, you might look for physical evidence. Are there footprints on the grass? A ramp or a ladder? Any cranes or elephant–moving equipment? You might take a walk all around the house and look closely for any changes. Whatever you find may tell you something about who might have put the elephant up there, and when it might have happened.

Conclusion: an opinion decided based on facts. In the broken window example earlier, your conclusion is realizing the baseball broke the window.

It might be a good idea to talk to some of the neighbors. Did they hear any strange noises? See any strange people? Maybe someone saw how the elephant was placed on the roof. It would also be a good idea to learn something about elephants. You might go to the zoo and talk to an elephant expert.

In other words, you would gather information by doing three things: looking, thinking, and asking. Finally, you would put together everything you learned and come to the best conclusion possible.

Even if you couldn't absolutely prove the *who* and the *how* of the elephant caper, you might get enough information to make a very good guess.

That's exactly how you would do your investigation of God. He himself may be invisible, but the evidence is not. You can look closely at several kinds of science. You can also talk to some really brainy scientists and experts who have already been collecting the clues.

The "Case" Books for Kids

Based on Lee Strobel's Gold Medallion Award–winning *The Case for Christ, The Case for Faith,* and *The Case for a Creator.*

Now those eye-opening bestsellers have been revised by noted children's author Rob Suggs for young people ages eight to twelve—the age when kids begin asking the complicated questions adults themselves struggle to answer. With a companion book—by prolific kids' author Robert Elmer—that gives real-life examples of ways to defend Christianity, these "Case" books are just right for kids who want to stand up for their faith in an unbelieving world.

Written in humorous, light-hearted prose perfect for kids this age, these books analyze the evidence and build compelling cases using historical facts, up-to-date scientific research, and true stories.

- *The Case for Christ for Kids* brings Jesus to life, addressing the miracles, ministry, family, and way of life of Jesus of Nazareth.

- *The Case for Faith for Kids* explains the most abstract articles of faith in ways kids understand.

- *The Case for a Creator for Kids* uses science to strengthen kids' faith, demystifying the creation of the universe with scientific evidence.

- For kids who are sure of their faith but not sure how to defend it, *Off My Case for Kids*—a perfect companion or a stand-alone piece—provides twelve real-life scenarios that empower kids to speak up when challenged.

Each book has plenty of visual interest, using line illustrations, callouts to define terms and phrases, and sidebars to help explain complicated concepts.

The Case for Christ
for Kids

Journalist Lee Strobel analyzed the evidence and built a compelling case for the existence of Jesus. Now his bestselling book has been revised—with kid-friendly terms, humor, and illustrations—to help kids really understand the life and times of Jesus Christ.

SOFTCOVER 0-310-71147-9

Available at your local bookstore!

zonder**kidz**

WILLOW
Willow Creek Resources